The Chinese Execution

for Carolyn and David
with love

Polly

A FEW AFTER WORDS FOR FRIENDS

After the structures of plots and arguments of rational
prose and the once conventional rhymes and rhythms of
poetry have been discarded as unsuitable reflections of our
social, political and spiritual worlds as they fall into
fragments; after we have made little 'slice-of-life' word
parallels of that shapeless reality; after all that is there any
kind of order? Maybe. Maybe sensory overload, like
sensory deprivation, without imposed organization begins
to show the dynamic pattern of the mind in operation –
brooding over the vast confusion to make a syncretic whole
of it. Under enough pressure, enough longing to
understand, the psyche can invent an image, a set of
images in some sort of dynamic relationship, which will
account for all the fragments and draw them like iron
filings to a magnet. That psychic key often occurs as a
dream.

The dream of the Chinese execution is such a key. It was
experienced May 3rd, 1989 and written down in the middle
of the night and then written again in the morning. In the
third account, written the next day, the trauma emerges.
After a few days, another account considered meanings.
Events in my life were galvanized by the dream into a new
pattern: they are represented in the book by individual
poems and their relationship to the accounts of the dream
is shown by a line from the dream account which appears
going vertically up the page. Because the lines from the
stories of the dream are remembered, they are not always
exact. Those discrepancies shift emphases, crack the
cemented rationality of our everyday path, and are the
ground of generation of dandelions and oak trees, stories,
myths, poems. So they are not corrected.

What the dream meant in my own life, prophetically, was that my husband was dying. The dream-invented metaphor of decapitation suits a brain tumour well enough and the process of treatment, everything done according to prescribed procedures while the family 'stands by' is not unlike an Oriental ceremony. That Banff should be translated into the exquisite North American part of the imperial garden is apt too.

What the dream may have meant otherwise borders on the paranormal, or on science fiction and/or madness. Three days after the dream, quite by chance, I heard on the radio a report from the BBC that several Tibetan monks had been killed by Chinese soldiers as they sat outside their monastery. They were protesting that they had not seen their leader, the monk left in charge by the Dalai Lama, for several months. I knew that I had seen that man, that he was the man on trial, the Asian who was killed. What's more, I would know him anywhere. What can that mean? It's a coincidence. Or, because my own psyche was about to warn me of a personal disaster and the great disaster was parallel, and somehow known by me but not consciously, it all came together for that dream. Or, my personal tragedy paralleling the decapitation of the monk opened doors for me to 'be there', indeed to participate in those proceedings. At one point I actually thought the other witnesses, accomplished astral travellers, conscious of where they were and each of them unwilling to be the one whose signal killed the monk, got me, an inadvertent traveller, into the situation so that my gesture would be responsible for his death and the guilt would be mine. My rejection of the butterfly, that is, of spiritual involvement, was the very gesture that killed the monk. So much for spiritual reach and grasp and the edge of madness.

Polly Fleck

December 1993

THE CHINESE EXECUTION

POLLY FLECK

Wolsak and Wynn. Toronto

Some of these poems have appeared in *Blue Buffalo, Canadian Woman
Studies / Les cahiers de la femme, Dandelion, Waves,* and *Zest.* Others are
part of "The Coyote Series," which was performed at the Banff Centre
in 1989 against a background of incidental sound created for it by
Canadian composer Robert Rosen.

Special thanks to The Banff Centre and to Don Coles, the poetry editor
in the writers' program there, for his suggestions, his interest and his
friendship.
Thanks also to R. J. Fleck, composer at the Center for Computer
Research in Music and Accoustics at Stanford University, who created
background and soundscapes for some of these poems.

Author's photograph by R. I. Fleck
Typeset in Palatino, printed in Canada by
The Coach House Printing Co., Toronto.

The publishers gratefully acknowledge support by
The Canada Council and The Ontario Arts Council.

Wolsak and Wynn Publishers Ltd.
Don Mills Post Office Box 316
Don Mills, Ontario, Canada, M3C 2S7

Canadian Cataloguing in Publication Data

Fleck, Polly, 1933-
    The Chinese Execution

Poems.
ISBN 0-919897-34-7

I. Title.

PS8561.L43C55 1993   C811'.54   C93-093911-5
PR9199.3.F54C55 1993

PAUL DUNCAN FLECK

1934 - 1992

My spring's warm sun and summer's
wonder – my white winter's
memory
and
icon over my unknown ever
after

CONTENTS

The Chinese Execution (I)

THE CHINESE EXECUTION (I)

On Monday night, May 3rd, I saw a man put to death. A ceremonial execution in an ancient imperial garden carefully remembered. A garden shifting like a still sky. The Canadian consul at Beijing had an invitation for several of us to be witnesses. And so we dressed in garden-party clothes, elegant and correct, as if we had gathered to watch a game of croquet. ★ The man was brought out at a shuffle-run between two guards, the hand of one of them at the back of his neck, forcing him along. He was an Asian, forty or fifty years old, and wearing the maroon pajama of a chinese political prisoner. He was calm; stunned, or drugged, perhaps. The rest of the court, brilliantly costumed in their robes of office, took their places. One of these stepped forward and read from a great tasselled scroll – an interminable length of time – what I thought must be the prisoner's specific crimes. Did that official take a second scroll from an aide, or was it the second official who read the sentence? Only one of them was wearing the red leggings of an official of the imperial judiciary. That took less than two minutes. A pause. Then, at a signal from the distant mandarin, the prisoner was rushed toward the executioner. ★ But wait, the scene is important here. The action is played out in a middle ground, a flat grassy plain beside a stream with the point of an island just visible on the right. On that point of land is a small ornate gazebo. We are watching from a grove of maple trees with a row of hollyhocks – taller than I am – behind us. There are five of us Canadians, very still, like a tableau in a wax museum, hoping this ceremonial entertainment is not also a real execution, and waiting for the axe to fall. Waiting

11

THE SABBATH DAY

Early in the morning if you get up slow and
blanket the sleeping night around you, pad
out to the other room
the dog close behind you
squeaking his yawns, stretching, shaking out
the night. No sudden radio news,
no sad residue of dreams
                                unremembered ...

If you get up slow and easy and look out
an early fall morning through the kitchen door
over the dawn mist on the Vermilion Lakes ...

If you look up to Pilot Mountain as the sun
strikes her snow, and slide the door softly
so the mule deer only turn their eyes ...

At the end of August the world goes yellow.
Wild grass first, then feathery larches
lighting up the mountains. October turns
the white-green poplars yellow.
First frost whites out the green pines,
white-tops the yellow foothills where they
meet new snow above the tree-line, mists over
the cooling earth. If you step out
                                and breathe in ...

You breathe in the whole sky – the air
full of white mountains, shadowy lakes
 – filling up your chest to bursting,
catching in your throat
with the coming-home of it.

12

OLD BEADS

The forest trembled with last notes and our wild applause.
The traverse, along the mountainside and through the pines,
our way home full of talk and laughter and
stumbling on a root and the beads broke and scattered
everywhere and suddenly it was almost
dark. But we got them all
scooping them up with pine needles and little stones
But next day on the way back
two more
beads were in the path
another on the way home, and
the next day and the next   until
I remembered
Tunnel Mountain and Mount Rundle
yearn toward the Vermilion Lakes and tumble
small stones down to her, their syllables of love,
down to her wet green-marsh duck-busy
shore.

Stones rest for days, aeons, then loosen and fall a little way
further toward the lake. Some get carried around
in pockets awhile or in soft hooves
when deer move across the mountain but
always
mountains move to claim the marshy edges of lakes
to become less mountainous, to reach
lake level.

13

Beads were once bedes, prayers
now pounded round, burnished, and drilled
to be hung at the throat we sing from
universal   stone   syllables.
And my melted glass beads from
India and Italy, old-cut amber from the Baltic
– years darkening among grandmother's handkerchiefs –
ebony from Africa, turquoises
from Arizona, wood beads from
yesterday's hippies.
And one so old I
was afraid
to hold
it.

That's the one
I lost and will not find – on its way toward the lake,
the key for all mountains and lakes, DNA for destruction,
and recreation, the
final syllable

14

a garden shifting like a still sky

LES GRANDS JARDINS MANQUÉS

After my mother died, I used to work in her garden
– weeding flowerbeds, scaring off squirrels.
Sometimes I forgot she wasn't there.

Mother's garden had a careful cheesecloth net
over the ripe strawberries and little birds would get caught
under it and fly it up
in squawking circus-tent points as you ran out
to get berries for dinner. If you ran too fast
the sparrows might take a fit and die.
Well, that's what I thought, so I had to go out
slowly, talking to them all the way. "Okay little
birdies, here I come so get out of there. It's
okay, the cat's not here."

One day I showed the whole game to Aunty Mae
– ma jolie, ma jeune, ma belle Tante Mae –
and we folded the net back laughing at
'sparrow hysteria' and looking for the ripest
berries that let their stems go easily, the basket
between us. Then
she took my hand and told me she was dying. No,
she didn't say that, she only talked about her child,
Gail, getting married. She liked the young man,
the lovely wedding. But I knew. I knew.

My heart shrieked up against the net
of her careful words, and my hand was a small bird
panicking in her hand – I said
we should take the strawberries in then
out of the sun.

15

Full sunlight and the rites of morning.
Rain or snow
I
comb them out and set them on
their day's adventure and as they
clatter out each one puts down
his sleep-smooth face for me to kiss an ear
and he is gone to turn
the wheels of things that really matter, things done
out in the world beyond
the door I wave from, the door
I wait at. I fade back I
wander around feeding
plants, fish, turtles, budgie, the dog, her pups.

What?
Has my hearing sharpened? I have caught
dragon-antiphons beyond the banded ionosphere
and heard light shake in the sky.

16

we were in our garden-party clothes

The foyer of the old King Edward is elegant enough and they 'do teas'. The women star in their own lives there, always conscious of the camera. Quietly dressed, they pour tea well (elbows in, backs straight, feet together), and know how to ask after a companion's mother.

One is called to her car by a tumble of grandchildren, all noise – 'Cookie, please, Gram' – and a young blue-jeaned nanny. To another, her driver presents his compliments. They go out so quietly you can't get into their life-plot from here. One pouty-mouthed magazine cover is rushed at by a romance-novel lover who lets me know he missed his plane.

I respond with the open-mouthed admiration they want, a sort of naive cameraman and audience. I used to want to be the first one called, first-chosen in the life-game team, so I could hurry away, serious and preoccupied. That was my working-woman cameo. Now I pretend our privacy is cunningly protected by angelic surveillance so that no one ever observes our meetings.

Women of a certain age know their mothers and God are always watching so they stage their lives – show up on time correctly costumed, motivated, the part memorized – and look for the camera. But what if God doesn't care any more about the ritual tea ceremony in a suitable silk dress? What if all her longing is toward the starving grandchildren in Ethiopia? Yes, well let me write those King Edward ladies down in generous memory while I wait for you – knowing it is past tea-time.

brilliantly costumed in their robes of office

AT CALGARY AIRPORT

Back past the newsstand again where the
            Sun has the last portrait of Princess Grace
        her eyes are called Calm and Triumphant, her
                mouth is set firm, her chin
                    elevated, she looks
        toward the future in confident hope, like
    parade banners of Lenin, Bethune of China, or
                    Eva Peron.
                So the Sun says she
            must have known. The Sun offers
    her last words to a stranger on the inside pages.
            I don't want to know them.

                The plane – five hours late –
        went back to Toronto, something was
                    wrong.
                Once some
    aeronautics man beside me said the fuselage
        would hold on impact but we would
    not survive. 'We would be shredded, yah,
                shredded, cut to ribbons
        by flying stuff stored overhead, still in
                our seatbelts.' 'I see,'
            I said, 'Thank you.' I had
            some Beaujolais, then, at
            thirty-five thousand feet.

18

THE HOSPITAL MUSEUM CURATOR

Self-assured, scientific, he says
madwomen portray the same sexual fantasies
with boring regularity, always
attempting the Edvard Munch style,
so he offers only six of these
not only to prove his point but
to devote more space
to the amazing variety of subject matter
and style of the male inmates' work.
I look, of course, only at the six.

Sometimes I feel I am the descendant
of some woman-painter whose work
didn't even get to the wall
because it did not illustrate
the good doctor's theory of madness
in woman. That's what it is
always to be the subject of
someone else's inquiry.

19

OMENS FOR NO EVENT

At a stoplight across six lanes of traffic through
the cab window – leaving London for the North –
I see her fall to the pavement, her dress
buckling, white-gloved hands fluttering.
Ineffectual, her gentleman in morning dress
calls out to us but we are
too far away and the light changes.

In light spring rain hiking north in
the Lake Country to Wordsworth's cottage
in the crossroads at
Ambleside lay a white dove, her heart
cored out and set beside her still attached
by a skein of blood. She held me
convexed in her staring eye until I
looked where her outstretched wing
was pointing and saw
a woman watching me. A portrait.
No, she is looking through an antique frame
and the shop window, someone in my
image. A mirror? My mother? Another
dimension?

This morning below the library window
a white-breasted junco tricked by glass-reflected
forest and flying into it
is dead among the first dead
leaves of autumn there.
I remember
a flutter of gloves, a gesture of a dove's
wing and a sense of unknown though predestined
darkness invades me.

20

the stream, the island, the gazebo

BLOODY SUNDAY

He emerges sullen at noon
to go swimming, muttering
about leaving home if
parents object to friends
'sleeping over' – especially
a girl locked out by her mother
who never even
takes off her boots. Anyway she left
earlier by his window to go down
through soft morning woods,
the deer still sleeping there, and I
am made to feel
old, dirty-minded, boring,
because I asked. he goes.

Now
you come home angry that I
   let him go not knowing
   he was to play tennis with you.

You call your brother
   birthday wishes long distance –
   laughter and reassurances.
You call someone else to play tennis.
You say I need not come to lunch
   since I seem not to want to.
You go.

And it's too late to tell you I missed
   hearing the linguist on the Stoney
   oral tradition and the Beowulf
   to get home for this luncheon.
Too late to tell you about the girl
   going through the window into the woods.

O God I envy her, locked out by her mother,
   going moccasin-soft through the morning
   woods without a word
            when the night is over.

But wait. The scene is important here

THE PYTHON CLUB

We're early so we look in the shops. You admit
a weakness for Italian leather: a jacket of
bright wet-look python made to look like plastic
chemic-dyed over the endangered species marks,
like discreet designers' names
on denim-look silk jeans for millionaires
and their hunters able to spot real python
disguised as imitation. Exclusive, the Python Club.

We laugh. That is, we will not be sad, or wonder
how many pythons are left in the world, or how
many of us.

We find silk hibiscus more beautiful than real
flowers mirror-multiplied into infinity. We are
talking about time, the weather, clients,
golden boy directors, shooting schedules.
US-Plastics up from Missourah says Toronto
packaged right is as good as Cleveland.

Is that what he said?

Paula arrives – kisses and laughter.
The waiter removes the fourth place but
not before I remember her mother and look away
– trying to keep her image from transferring
to you. We are the survivors of the wrecks
of our lives, deaths and other sheddings.
That plastic-coated python
is preserved almost forever.

22

the small ornate gazebo

THE MAGIC LANDSCAPE

Light came through the forest
over the mountain sometime between
six and six-thirty in the morning while I
was writing, 'Thank you for the happy gabbling
dinner last night,' and revealed a deer
lying close-in near the house, night-sheltering
where I was sure she was even while
it was still dark. By seven when the sun
struck Pilot Mountain and gently avalanched
through the lodge-pole pines
she'd hardened into a rock for a day
of stillness. You can just make out her rump
lying down, a boulder
twilight will reanimate.

23

DAD'S SECRETARY: 1945

After the war her little red hat
sat on her forehead,
like a miner's lamp held on by
invisible wires, will power,
and dropped its
fly-speck veil down to her nose-end.
"Nifty," Daddy said.

Her black wool coat, red silk taffeta
inside, went swish-a-swish into
offices her perfume
had pried open and clouded into.

Her spike heels tapped grown-up code
in the marble rotunda right up to
the hall of big brass elevators
echoing back her typewriter's
clickety-clack. Her red nails clicked
on our table, too, as
she told us, Mother and me,
about glamour and 'sheek'.
"Indeed," Mother said.

She met important people for cocktails
in New York when it was half-naughty'
said, 'Dawh-ling'
to 'business & professional' women, and
maybe to a man. And she let
her party-careless laughter, loud enough
to seem at home in the place, run
Hollywood-round the chrome-slick
Rendezvous.

24

Now her recorded voice, brisk as ever
bone-brittle, manicured,
wants me to leave
'Name, Number, Nature of Business.'
I can hear her fingernails
tapping right up to the beep.
"A real crackerjack," Dad used to say.

25

a tableau in a wax museum

ST. JAMES'S PARK

Lying among Lovers, shading
under the magazine section laid against
my unbelieving eyes, I
refocus the page of Sunday terror.

"teasing little strips of flesh
with great skill and a straight razor, with
mounting excitement, wet red thongs drawn
off their chests and they opened up from
shock" – words choking out words,
spilling blood and gibberish, stilling
into ooze and whispers, into
satiate after-passion sighs into silence.

His first kill, virgin blood, at sixteen, he
shot a man buried
up to his mouth in
sand, still screaming, 'No'. He felt sick.
He says so   and he
is here. The South American is here in
St. James's Park every Sunday,
armed, his ethnic male necessity, among
lovers.
In the sun, this assassin, and in
transition. The Times
assures its readers he is going
away
to Canada, to
marry a virgin and raise
children. He turned in his adoptive father
who buried men in sand to train him.

Sometimes home-sickness is a knife struck,
sudden
heart-attack in St. James's Park.
Oh
Canada, CANADA.

26

The Chinese Execution (II)

THE CHINESE EXECUTION (II)

It was a theatre-piece, a pageant, of course. The prisoner-actor, so calm and noble, the scene so beautifully staged in the North American part of the garden. But why are we asked to attend, we Canadians? Has the Asian something to do with us? An Innuit? Spying? Impossible! If it were real then our being expected to watch the execution would be our punishment and a warning that interference in Chinese politics will not be tolerated. ★ Oh Christ I know the prisoner! My heart moves toward him in an ancient loyalty and I know the execution is real. Under the staged imperial ornamentation a real condemned man will really die here. We wait. The prisoner waits. The black-helmeted executioner waits. ★ A butterfly appears. He is in the colours of the hollyhocks behind me, the colours of my party dress. He loves me; lights on my hem and is swished off and lands on my sleeve. The consul's executive assistant at my left moves her head from side to side almost imperceptibly. She means me to be still. ★ I contemplate my white leather shoes, heels sinking into the combed lawn. The wind stirs. The butterfly clings as the dress moves and flutters. The assistant warns me with a sharp look. I look away – at the gazebo. I see it is a sedan chair with the carrying rods removed and someone is inside it. – Now the consul moves between his assistant and me and whispers that we are waiting for our host, Chi Louw, the supreme official, to give the signal from the flowing-stream safety of the island. He will drop the point of a small ornamental sword at the window of the red-lacquered gazebo: that way he will see the execution occur immediately after the conjunction of certain planets.

29

A big circus lady with yellow hair and flame-tattered spangles who swallowed fire, when I was fifteen and had not been anything anywhere promised me her brother's magic if I could 'jazz up her act' with the word-toys I played with. I watched her brother's magic. I told her, 'You pretend the fire is in you, comes out of you, the spiel I make you about the fire-dragon hidden under your bed, about the symbiotic secrets he fire-feeds you mouth to mouth, will by night softly resuscitate the midday midway hocus-pocus. The fire you spit at the crowd will catch those rubes by their lobes and drag them in.

Merlin-like the vision worked her a magic. She made herself a mystery; spiel, incantation, spell. But the wild boy I loved and watched was not her brother to offer. She laughed that the fire-drake was hers – could not be called back, that she could say, 'Go away kid,' and she did. Then I shook out the picnic cloth of that summer's feast – ants and crumbs I left to each other and basketed the rest into attic chaos. Now a postcard 'Nessymonster' falls out. On it 'thinking of you' from the false brother. Charred spangles, summer splinters: these cut like a mother's tongue all your life when you're young.

Almost old and academic, among colleagues, old Scotch, cocktail banalities and dark Renaissance convolutions, a professor with many eyes and a dry voice, a non-believer in dragons although his income depended on what they said to him, told me literary dragons have names for annotation or are mere manifestations of psychoses. 'Clearly, alas, this dragon of yours is one such.' The wild boy was at my ear like Ariel with the summer's thunder. He called out, 'MOGADOR.' The fire-drake flashed his great wings round the hall from wall to wall. Split-tongued he sang out – 1844 – the Bled Siba where the poets died in fire, unheard.

It was a theatre-piece, a pageant

I caught the fire from his mouth, the circus-spangled lady in his scales. He covers me like stars falling. We are all one creature. We sing with one voice, Circus Lady, dragon and I. Some men speak with tongues of angels and some sing among madmen and poets translating utterances, hoping to strike truth for fire-watchers and other listeners to lies. Poets sing about days poets remember. Mogador, Great Dragon of the Mind's Despairing, Guardian of Word-hoards, sing to me and I will sing the antiphon.

31

There was too much between that dog and me. I kept saying to him, 'I always wanted a dog like you, you grisly old love, but I can't take you where I'm going today. You wait and I'll be back.' More and more places won't have dogs. And what I really meant was I didn't know how I got into this fix, being led out every day by a dog and tied to the house. And dogs always hear what you mean so one day when I let somebody else take him for a walk, he got his leg broken so he couldn't walk so fast and he'd be less trouble.

I taught him the trick of living so close. I broke my ankle when he was a pup and my life was falling apart – bones are made of love and caring, you know – and he lay on the cast to keep it warm, and when the cast came off, he licked the mangled foot to heal it. When it was his turn, I held him in my arms but I couldn't heal him. We needed a miracle. We wanted me to love him better but I couldn't think how to do that.

He stayed as close as he could. When I sat at my desk he would lie under my feet, his old bones thumping down on the cold wood floor, so he could go to sleep knowing I was still there. He would lick my ankle from time to time – sort of 'in passing' as if he remembered when it was broken. Then he got cancer in the leg – there was no bone left in it – a crippled dog who didn't try to get up on the bed any more or sit where people sit in the car because their damn clothes are so important.

Now he doesn't have to be walked by anybody. He doesn't snore and wake me or bite my foot to get let out in the middle of the night. He doesn't even have to be fed, except by my tears that feed his memory. Although sometimes at night I hear him bark at the door and go to let him in.

32

The prisoner-actor was so calm and noble

THEY PACKED ALL NIGHT

He left with all his stuff early
in the morning and she decided
to make bread to take
her mind off his leaving like that
and because she couldn't sleep
and didn't want to waste the morning.

By ten, when she was
pummelling and working her dough
the second time, he came in
through the front. She hadn't heard
him, he was just there.

She asked if he'd missed the plane.
He nodded. She told him to go to bed
he looked tired, grey, changed. He
smiled at her sadly, like a little boy,
                and went down the hall.

She remembered how he loved to have
baby oil after his bath, how he used to
smile and coo and reach out to her
when she rolled him side to side.

She worked the bread, shaped it, smoothed
it with flour, laid a linen tea towel over it
and set it out carefully to rise.

She sat down then, at her kitchen window
to watch the shadows of hollyhocks sundial
across the grass   and woke up
hearing the phone ringing and surprised
to find her face was wet.

33

we are expected to watch the execution

'I am old,' she thought, 'older than the
blessed hills' she heard her mother
say in her head, 'my eyes water.'

She picked up the phone, 'Yes, she
would wait for them,' put it down
carefully and went to look in his room.

34

A STRATHROY GARDEN

She can't see. Her hands
in front of her face are only
shapes there because she knows she's
holding them up, remembering
what they looked like. You see what you
know is there, what you want to see,
and we are not to celebrate the sight
that's left. That's hardly a
medical victory.

The Japanese cherry was a picture caught
in a slant of early morning sun against the
grey wood fence, and the white magnolia
hung down its branches of great blooms
the day she left the cottage for
hospital. She stared and stared.
They were never so beautiful,
never. They knew. They were
saying good-bye. And now
the water lilies will be coming on.

Later in the spring the jay will shriek
warnings and swoop down at her
from the magnolia where
he nests and keep her
out of the garden.

Tibetan monks whose ancestors
prophesied Russian tanks moved
out from the Potala into
mountain caves certain holy
artifacts.

The first road block was that they did
not dwell in meditative forests, and led
no one, therefore,
into the caves by way of mountain paths
read in the mind.

The last barricade. The porter-monk
swung himself over a gorge, thinking
himself UP
onto the ledge and into
the cave – the dead weight trajectory
altered by taking thought.
It lifted him. No soldier-engineer
following
would think a monk could do that
so the holy caves are safe.

In the year of the Wood Creatures, I
was born, and married
in the Year of the Iron Dragon in
another part of the forest
in diffused sunlight, modulated by
passing clouds and knowing about
the safety of caves, the value
of thinking myself up.

36

interference in Chinese politics is not tolerated?

THE YORK CYCLE CRUCIFIXION
(UofT Front Campus, Fall)

We wanted a good view of the Crucifixion so we
missed the end of the trial and cut across
the old campus. University of Michigan did it; got it
by lot. Four Michigan line-backer Roman soldiers
lashed a thin nearly naked man
to a cross of four by fours and raised him into
a square iron bracket at the end of a wagon,
that's all.
                        And there he was.

We wanted to see the Crucifixion. It was raining
so we were under newspapers on bleachers
Michigan supporters all around us. Engineering
had figured it out on paper but lashing his arms
over the crossbeam he loosened the ropes trying
to help them. The corporal snarled,
"For Chrissake leave it alone." "Right on Man,"
we shouted. To raise the cross the biggest man braced
the foot and two others walked it upright. The
fourth man walked backwards palms up toward the chest
of the Jesus-actor till he was upright. We cheered.
The soldiers bowed.
                        And there he was.

Wait. We were looking at the Crucifixion.
It was raining. We heard the Lieut-Governor
was coming. Michigan around us thought that was
real 'med-eye-evil,' really Canadian, the Queen's
representative at the Crucifixion, a U.S. senator,
would be at the Resurrection. We got rowdy
waiting like that. Then there was real thunder
to enhance their drum-roll as we watched
the soldiers lift the cross straight up

O Christ, I know the prisoner

two and a half feet, groaning and gasping
into the iron bracket. It dropped into
place. We cheered. The Jesus-actor
cried out as his arms took the jolt. Agony crossed
his face. His crown of thorns slipped sideways
and cut him. He was trembling, blood and rain
running down his face and shoulders.

So that was the Michigan Crucifixion, how it went.
It went deep. He cried out. Somebody said, "Okay,
it's finished: get him down." The Roman soldiers
squared up to defend the cross: Michigan supporters
outnumbered us. We waited huddled under newspapers,
not looking. The rain fell heavier now. It got dark.
Jesus began to shake with cold, his whole body
and he cried out, "My God why hast Thou forsaken me?"
                              And there he was and we were with him.

The sun came out for the Resurrection. A Michigan
senator and Mrs. McGibbon were there and Higgins,
a graduate student, found our Jesus-actor having a beer.
Was it the real thunder made it real? The unintended blood?
                              Michigan got the performance prize.

38

IMAGES: A SONNET DECONSTRUCTION

Yesterday morning a snowy egret in flight
over the pond   reflected only
a gesture of wings catching
into my eyes.
This morning while you sleep, your arms
winged out like flight on the white sheet,
that silver wing thing catches me
up to you. My heart lifts off

in sudden joy   and settles again
                              in you.
Down long years snowy egrets will stand
self-reflecting in the still dark pond
                    And I will
watch   wanting
              sudden wings,
                        joy.

39

NIGHT MUSIC: OCTOBER

Oh God I hear you Coyote –
over Dungeons and Dragons the guttural hum
and rumbling of male voices
downstairs,
over the forced air long-dragon breathing of the furnace,
pipes and floorboards cracking
asymmetrical percussion,
over the dog snoring and dream-barking
at my feet.

Outside the night is colder
cold enough for Coyote to crack the glass sky
re-align memories
of other nights, other voices.

Toward morning   a long howl
along the trench of the night will wake me into
the running day.

40

It was nothing – so small a thing.
She saw him down the street and called out
he turned, turned back and went on
– like a stranger who hears his name
in another city and turns around
and turns away again.

Was she wrong? No, his walk, his beautiful
ugly heliotrope sweater. The street shifted
suddenly into off-true. Not seeing
her and getting closer to the corner he
would turn and be out of sight.

She runs back through the offices
to the car and drives round to find him
– or that parallel stranger,
the one who doesn't know her – no sign
of him further along.

She remembers yesterday he didn't know
her voice on the telephone – 'Who do you
think it is?' Then she starts to shiver,
thinks of crying. She is an abandoned child
again – exploding in anger – mad
because he is leaving her.

The child says, 'Alright leave me – I'll
be alright and I won't cry. You're trying
to make me cry? Well I won't. You saw me.
You did. You're pretending you don't know
me – so you're going. Why? I
don't care why. I don't care.'

There he is coming out of the drugstore.
Yes he'd seen her – thought she'd know where
he was going – had she forgotten? Everything is
alright then. No. A desperate worried child
already fading is calling out
something she cannot hear.

a real condemned man will really die

41

THE HOTEL

Two in the morning the desk clerk
says I did not reserve
today. 'Someone else, yesterday.'
He finds it, a room, a key. He watches me
still angry
until the elevator doors close, a woman about
whom there was some non-
trouble.

Long curved corridors, the Enterprise, night-dimmed,
light at intervals where four doors
huddle together.
My door is open. Someone is in bed.

Back
along the perimeter track, tangent into
the elevator. The desk
does not say he does not
believe me, but he is not amused
at this silliness. He offers a room with
no key.   The bellman will unlock it for me.
I will not leave it, he says, and they laugh. I think they
mean that it is too late for me to go
anywhere else, anyway.

42

A WOMAN'S CIRCLE

Sometimes when I walk into a room where
he is I feel I
am standing trial for something
unspecified I omitted to do.

No, that's a big step: I
used to set
all my inadequacies against all
he expects of me.
I used to set the dinner table
early if dinner were going to be late
to avoid the silent treatment but he would
look at his watch, sigh and rap
his fingers on the padded chair arm,
anyway. Now
he suspects there's someone else. There is. It's me, I
got up off my knees and began to walk.

But sometimes when I walk ...

43

she warns me with a sharp look

ALONE IN VILLEFRANCHE

Home alone
she puts on his reading glasses
 – strangely unclear for her –
to look through his eyes,
                    and she sees things.

Every time they went out to eat at
bottle-and-candle-stub places
the candle burned out between them. She saw
that as an omen. Tried not to but the
eye strain gave her a headache,
and made her eyes cry.

When they walked on the shore – Prospero's
Island is out there
but you can't get there now –
they lit candles in Cocteau's
Chapelle de Saint Pierre to walk on water.
She saw his longing in her heart.

He went away then back to Canada
and it rained two days
 – his dark thoughts down through his
reading glasses. She knows his focus
better than her own.

44

AFTER DINNER AT TRAPPERS'

He gave me back my ring
without ceremony.

Sister Ruth had worked away at it
working the soft flesh through, resting
his hand then – elevated to reduce swelling –
willing the gold band over the knuckle.
It waited for me. She said I put it
on him, I should take it off.
So I did, without thinking.

And put it on my index finger
for safety. I took it back.
He sighed and moved deeper into sleep
loosed from me. Free. Sometime after midnight
then
Earth's shadow moved across the face
of the full and cloudless moon.

45

at the conjunction of certain planets

The Chinese Execution (III)

THE CHINESE EXECUTION (III)

He told us that a mandarin does not take the death of any individual lightly, that we were waiting for this man, whose breeding and education have prepared him for it, to determine the moment for execution best suited to the protection of the state, and to drop the sword. It would not be much longer since these events were scheduled to send the prisoner into eternity at a moment when there was least chance of his becoming a hero-martyr, of his fathering civil unrest. ★ The butterfly moved. Why did I think I had to get rid of him – as if it had been my policy over the last thousand years but I wanted this one to go free? The air itself went dead calm. Were we breathing in unison? The red-gaitered official, the axeman, the guards, and the prisoner began to sway together as if painted on a silk panel. Then the little window was open and the ceremonial sword could be seen, its point raised. ★ The butterfly opens his wings. I slide the white-gloved fingers of my right hand up to my left shoulder. He steps on. I look to see if either the consul or his assistant is watching and then arc the butterfly downward across my dress and cast him into flight. The mandarin makes the same gesture exactly with the little sword and the execution is on. Fast. Sleight-of-hand. The guards run the prisoner up to the axeman, throw him onto his knees, his face, as the axe goes up. I shut my eyes. ★ I opened my eyes to see the grey silk shoulders of the consul blocking my view. As we left, the guards were putting the folded body – it looked boned and gutted – into a square box and the axeman arranged the head to rest in the centre. I had given the signal to kill the prisoner. The consul said we could go. We stepped into another part of the garden.

49

LEAVING BANFF

Fast-moving clouds strobe-light the moon,
wake up giants out of old mountains
roaring and moaning.

Coyote skirts the edge
of lamplight at the bus stop.
He hears something in the wind
sits back to answer
                spots me watching
                          moves on
                      loping sideways
                                nose down,
over the dark train tracks into forest
on the far side.

Bus tires crease down Highway #1,
drown out the windraging
of mountains and make them
silent actors on the moonsilver screen
of my window.

Mountains relax into hills.
Then flatlands where the windwhine
is too high for human ears. This is
what Coyote hears, is what
we feel catch in the throat as we
begin to say
something trivial, human.

50

We arrange ourselves
in a Japanese prospect simply, in
designed and austere
luxury.

Four of us watch four raccoons
in the low branches of
the great pruned maple. They watch us.
We are a circle of eight creatures, all
silent. Then you ask me,
courteously,
questions to be answered in two words,
haiku, no stories, no going the long way
through our lives or even into
the tone and texture of our being
with you and contemplated by
four parallel raccoons.

You indicate decorously that you
are tired and we leave
through the front hall with the
minimal ceremony due close
relatives.

If only I had imagined I
wanted to speak to you
about something else ...

Or if there had been only two
raccoons, or the Zen-calm
had not silenced us so soon; or had
it not been so late
I might have uttered some word
in the structure of
that moment.
Or heard
one.

We are waiting for this man

EVE, SOCIAL WORKER

Five o'clock and thank-God-it's-Friday
Uncle Sam's Motel, Niagara, ladies' room
British Red Coat lips on and …

'You bitch,' a crack, pain, the floor
getting closer, someone saying,
'She's drunk.' She whispers/yells, 'Help me.'

X-rays can't find the 'alleged' bullet.
No one saw a woman, a gun, a psychologist
reports, 'Wound self-inflicted – nailfile maybe –

to get attention. She will admit this or be
charged with 'public nuisance' and lose
her job. Her mother tells them she

agrees to say so. Her mother tells her
'It's a man's world after all.'
Three days later in Toronto, pain.

A video-taped police-monitored procedure
pulls a bullet out of her pelvic bone – too late
Niagara police cannot repoen a closed case

– closed, recorded, and reshaping
Statistics Canada, the whole system
leaning toward the duplicity of women,

would self-destruct. Red-coat red lips on
out into the singles bar, 'Hey, you're the one
who faked up that film clip – Hey,

I'm on your side, lady.'

Instinct
drives the littler bitch to chase
creatures into their burrows.
If she can't find her way out
she dies. She digs
round in circles until
somebody sent to find her
treads overhead and caves in
her earthen roof and she
suffocates.

So you get a new bitch,
larger or thicker-coated
or pregnant. Her instinctive
burrowings internalized,
she surfaces in the new life.

The male when he
wants the underground creature
digs straight down. If it isn't there,
it can't be got at, or it
can't exist. That's what he says,
and he's alive to say it.

53

And drop the sword

SOUNDING THE NIGHT

The night is full of light,
a sound cone of far-off crickets,
the whine of tires creasing the highway on
the known world's rim
rides out its
steel-belted mountain-amplified
modulations and
fades.

Some creature, Coyote maybe,
cracks a twig, dog growls
under the bed.
Into the night's hum I say, "shhhs".
He adds his tail-percussion.

The silent-running moon
reads her score in the glassy lake, conducts
us toward morning.

54

AC FLT. 911 (28/1/86: 11:35 AM)

A long spiralling cloud is rolling down
  flat-paint sky. And over here
    turning particles of light
     are slow-falling from
     high up all the way
        down to the sea
and levelling out over
  long concave arcs
   of sand beaches.

That shore was hollowed out a hundred thousand
  years for its beaches and headlands now
    to parallel the drifting arcs of
     that slow-falling structure
         of cloud.
     The curvature of the earth
       concaves the sky.
    Winds shape waves
      rolling in.
   And this cloud-written
     cipher spinning out
  against blue sky is
unwinding the shape
    of creation.
    A perfect day.
Flight attendants hand out   the Miami Herald
  Toronto Globe. The captain tells us
    Challenger blew up a few seconds ago
    two minutes into take-off.
     The vertical spiral cloud
      starboard is the vapour trail.

  Apparently there are no survivors.
   You survived. Those sunlit
   particles of gold drifting
  down and turning slowly
through our inner atmosphere
  are phonemes and crystal syllables of
    new-made heroes, of eternal sagas unwinding.

his chance of being a hero-martyr

THE CHALLENGER EFFECT

Since Challenger's corkscrew cloud
rolled down
into the sea, and reamed out
my inner eye, my life is in eclipse.
That cloud screws down everything;
new moments, present laughter, bright hopes
too soon
spiral down
into a glassy sea of
time past, another dimension.

Faces I love are like long-dead loves
returning in dreams, saying
gruff old muttered
stuff like, "What's the matter Pup?
Are y'down-hearted?
And
in the gentle cadence of
my child's humming with his ear phones on
I can hear my mother
singing long ago. Her rich mezzo floats out
"Rocka my soul in the bosom of Abraham
Oh, rocka my soul."

And
Challenger is set in the sky, a constellation
of seven stars lighting our
pilgrimage in space.
A
pillar of cloud
for us now.
In the coming night a pillar of
fire.

a butterfly opening his wings

RIVER ICE

I used to walk on the ice
across the river –

like walking on the water –
until a woman came up under the ice
her hair drifted out around her
and looked at me.

At first she was unfocussed
staring with dead eyes. I would see
her once a winter, just a dead person
it would be useless to report.

Now she comes up under me
whenever the ice is clear.
She stares at me, she
wants out and I am
supposed to do that for her.

It's no use telling her to wait
till spring or summer when
the ice melts,
she has to get out through me.

I don't believe it. The woman
in the river accuses me of
her death but she is
– in whatever sense she is dead –
a suicide. The doctor says I
am not responsible for her getting out.

I look for her anyway,
even in summer among swimmers
I watch for someone on the edge of them
watching me. I want her to wave to me
as she goes under.

57

In a plate-glass reading corner magnified spring sun
stuns, lenses me up. The book falls
from listless hands. Friar Bacon's magic burns off
drifting pages. I want you
to appear.

All day I watch among steel shelves
extending themselves from roots
in concrete through four levels of
composition floors, soundproof
steel ceilings – *litera* to *anagogia*
searching out Kermode on John Donne
"contrapuntal velocity of thought"
rising, descending, rising again
in steel boxes among
strangers with the magic stare
through me. Where
are you?
                    If light bends,
Love, you can turn to me.

58

AT THE CLINIC

You slept all night. I watched
changes in the sky – moonset
and the stars
appearing and fading out again
along the edge of first light –
drifting out the dark hours
in the rhythm of your breathing
us out into the cool sky
 – till morning when you woke up
contained again, bewildered.

We go down to the clinic –
hard light on cold terrazza
walled round by patient eyes.
Nurse-learned, labelled laser-monitored
cancer is distanced, understood
 – a little science project to hold
on to survivers' stories, a positive
attitude. Holding on for dear life
the sick become as little children
holding on too tight to someone
who brought them – first day of school –
among programmed strangers.

But each day they breathe deeper into
the disease, closer than hungry lovers
breathing out the fear of it, breathing in
enthusiasm, breathing out love,
breathing in obsession until breath is
stilled – ecstatic infinite
moment. So you are leaving me.

59

The mandarin makes the same gesture

Suddenly a white-coat clipboard
condescension stoops to know me ... 'Not me
I brought someone.' I stand up free of her
– and you. So I betray you, Love,
tricked into choosing life separate, alone.
Patients who hear me turn away so I
won't see their longing to be able
to choose. They turn away too because
'terminal' is so exclusive a club,
the word itself is not even breathed.

We will drive back into the mountains
that used to be our 'home safe' place
and another night of
watching the dark starred sky, hearing
your even breathing pulsating
into the universe.

60

COYOTE FIRE

                              Some nights when
                         Coyote circles the clearing
                    edge of my campfire
                    closing in
               as the light dims, as
          the dying fire cracks,
          a twig snaps right,
I count to five slowly,
                                        ONE
          TWO   in
     sudden
               eyes glint
                    firelight THREE   two
                         sideways as
                    he arcs behind me   one
                         counter-clockwise FOUR
                              a leaf   out
                         whispers, I hear   two
                         breathing-in,   one
a shadow drifts
past the gap where the moondim
pewter of the lake - silvery grey on past grey –
          reaches into infinity. Count
                              five again, no,

                    I will be still,
               not breathing, watching the
          stealthy night pass and the silent
                    arc of the moon
                    going down.

     61

I had given the signal to kill the prisoner

I am a stone
still, breath-held, walled in
by wild longing fear of
him – watching for him
– a still shape among wind-shifting
shadowy leaves,   a breathing
shadow when there is no wind –
What if
I find him
in the morning imprinted in
the ashes of my fire.

62

I had given the signal to kill the prisoner

The Chinese Execution (IV)

THE CHINESE EXECUTION (IV)

The horror of the thing has no place to light. It must be a pageant. It must be. That way we can avoid the shock and weeping would be childish, like someone unused to theatre who thinks the struck-down actor is really dead. It would be easy to fake that death: as the axe falls, the actor rolls into a trench and is replaced by a doll in his costume to be rolled into place. The motion detaches its papier-mache head. But a ceremony which wants an inadvertent gesture from me? ★ It's a ritual performance – like an *in absentia* excommunication from the Church, using a stand-in. Or, the actor may be honoured to play the part of a man despised in his time under the imperial court and put to death, now revered in this regime. Remember the Crucifixion in the little German town? That sort of thing. No. It was real. Then she remembered the butterfly. How he loved her and voice began to well up in her. And power. She decided that this was an emperor's clothes story: everybody so anxiously fooling himself that it had been some sort of theatre while she alone had faced the fact that a human being had been killed. Dead, translated, and lives still. ★ The other woman, the one at the ceremony, still hopes some Chinese officials will meet them, introduce them to the actors for their congratulations. She even hopes the consul will say he believes some of his group thought it was real – meaning her – and the Canadians will laugh and the Chinese will be happy at such a genuine compliment from persons in so unsophisticated and diverse a culture. But nobody met them after the execution. She could not even remember going home.

65

THE INSTITUT

You climb up stone steps between cool-shuttered houses,
garden walls limbs of blossoming apricot lean over
their gates slyly ajar show you an old dog nosing
around a woman with expresso, a tennis court.
Then you huff and squeeze along a street
narrow with abandoned cars, the flow
of morning traffic down to the sea
and get to the gate, "l'Institut
de Français," too breathless
to say it.

A white villa – a pre-revolutionary dream of paradise –
way up
hundreds of steps through her orange grove and long terraces
of roses, arbours of grapes, red azalea, purple clematis
drawing you heart-pounding up the greystone steps
sweating against the perpendicular landscape,
to look out at last to the flat gold
Mediterranean Sea where the breathless
sun glides up behind you gathering
your last strength toward
his zenith.

The stairs last turn and straight ahead the alcoved head
of Bacchus above the new grapes smiles, open-mouthed,
salacious, stone blind, staring at the flatgold sea.
Green-steep garden, white villa go flat in slant
sun, a stage-set painted on the thick gold air
As if you could breathe in deep and pull
that veil against you and the hot
thick-lipped god would suck
your mouth out to sheathe
his foreign tongue
thrust in.

66

CAT CHANGING

She thought about her cat, used to call her
'Ali', Alley Cat for honesty, then Cubby
for 'lion cub' as she got to know her, as
the cat got bigger.

She'd roll over and over on her bed,
attack and pounce, confidence
of the predator at play, purring loudly
claws retracted.

The women came to the door that day
six of them, mouths set, clearing throats.
'Are you a delegation?' she laughed,
blinking. And they were.

They saw that she was alone, puzzled and
meaning to be conciliatory. They pushed
forward. She was a little frightened.
Then she heard the cat and turned.

Growling deeply, softly, nose down,
ears pinned back, the floor trembling,

she's huge, a lioness, and her name
is El Alamein.

The women, feeling they may have come
at a bad time, offer to find their way

out.

The actor is replaced by somebody in his costume

COYOTE AS POET

Full moon and the freight train's vertical scream
howls like pain in coyote's bones, growls
in the ground under
his paws, rumbles like hunger in his gut,
opens
his throat in long involuntary
lamentations,
hollowing out the valley, the caverned
pools and rivers sounding
through canyons inside
Sulphur Mountain.

And Coyote's long cry finds the cave and
melts the seal where childhood dragons sleep –
and a deeper place where
monsters from the old age
of the race wait for
Gabriel's Horn. Shut up Coyote
it is not yet time.

A ceremony which wants my gesture, my voice?

HER NEW HUSBAND WENT ELABORATELY TO BED

"Good-night, good-night".
Her new husband went elaborately to bed.
We sat across the table
from each other, with
white wine and the long-windowed
moonlight contained us
        and the moon-charged lake
        was catching at her shore.

He came back to show me
his bridegroom-new dressing gown.
'Very smart.' He went to bed again.
We talked,
sounding the flood of moonlight
through the sleeping cottage,
the deep lake curling along her shore.

He padded round the kitchen,
warned about white-wine moonlight, got
milk and cereal all by himself.
She told me
her father's last words to her.
Everything my father expected of me
was understood, was done; there was
nothing to say, at the end.

He went ceremoniously to brush his teeth.
"I am going to bed now". He closed the door.
We remembered the Strathdees, the children,
we said, 'accidental'
                and the cold lake worried at
                        her granite shore.
 – soft, soft, something not said
about her old husband in his wild
bad-tempered, drunken, handsome
days – where she saw that I
was not the 'other woman' and I saw
she had forgiven me anyway.

69

Everybody anxiously fooling himself

Her new husband came back;
"Time to be tucked up in beddy-byes".
He closed the door, sharply this time.
She was like a ghost. Then he
was rapping the wall, "s.o.s. s.o.s."

"Good night", "Good night"
we whispered and the moon climbed
                        higher in the cloudless sky.

70

DECONSTRUCTING CHRISTMAS DINNER

Dad remembers Aunty Kate Baines of his youth
who told him he would hear one of her boots
hit the floor upstairs after she had said,
'Good-night' but he was not to hear the second
boot. He would kiss sweet Milly B. on the cheek,
step out, 'Good-night Aunty Kate' and slam
the door, doff his cap
to the lace-curtained neighbours and
saunter home along Greenfield Street as
late as ten-thirty on a summer night, 1909.

It was 1899 before he realized his uncle
always missed Santa coming through
the conservatory skylight with his big sack.

1990, yesterday, a playwright came late
to Christmas dinner – just out of bed – brought
his unannounced friend, her split lip taped,
hair a fashionable mess, looked at none of us,
pouty mouth and spoke to no one, elbowed him
and poked at her plate till he said 'turnip',
or 'stuffing' and turned back
to his conversation on the other side.

When they left he said she's an actress.
So why couldn't she 'improvise' a Christmas
dinner the way it was and talk to us.

71

It's a ritual performance

It looked smaller outside. Snow
shaken off, bud worm tips pinched off,
bottom branches
sawn off, and shaped into
stand and door wreath –
hand over branch
stinging needles, sap sticking
smell of mountain forest
everywhere
she wrestled up fourteen feet
into the point of the roof, from tree into
forest spirit, a wild
entanglement of the house,
iron-booted and tied up
to iron railings, landing and stair, with
my scarf. I sat down then   under her branches
we made our bond.

I worked all morning alone
against the ingrain of
world-death,
against
famine in Ethiopia,
– God keep this house – new lights
for dead ones. At noon I strung the lights from

A
silver star
hand-made at home
against greed sparkling in
the eyes of TV winners of things;
– God keep this house – and round the tree

round and round
all the way
down
lights I strung against terror
in the news at noon; old cracked ornaments from
Gramma's house mended with family

The actor may be honoured to play the part

hand-me-down
stories about strong women
who gave us, our childhood Christmas magic
who put candy canes for children
where they could reach
faded paper
garlands,
strung branch to branch and winding down
around the tree, against
false trees,

Christmas decor and real
trees felled to make the New York papers –
God keep this house, this country, this forest
safe.

A ritual dancer, then,
weaving in and out, and winding
round the tree I flung
new tinsel she caught in her branches
reaching out to me, setting
herself
against plastic trees, restaurant turkey, against
Florida Christmasses
loneliness – me and this tree being alone.

And I sang my mother's song from long ago,
"Oh que la mere est bel-le, oh que
le Chris-te est beau."
So I was not alone.

It was done at 4:30. When it
was almost dark the great tree sprang to light.

All the years strung back further than
I remembered were lit up and
stung deeper than the needling
tree. I sat down beside her
liquid lights
unshadowing Christmasses.

Autumn is a dry-crack clarity in the air
before leaves are burned, before
snow falls.

Sharp winds like spine-running harps
pirouette bright costumed
shivers of leaves.

Leaves
rattling down churn up inside, re-align
unfocused dim
memories into too sharp intensities:
Dad, small all in grey in front of a snowdrift
bright day, his eyes so sudden blue
the whole sky was coming through his head.
Some forgotten question with no answer lit up our
tree-branch-sustained-by-root-system
living. Now the leaves are falling.
Tears come into eyes suddenly like the flares
of matches set to
bonfires.

74

THE DAY AFTER NEW YEAR'S

By noon the dry tree
is stuck in grey driveway snow
shot through with tinsel
worried by the wind
                    rag ends of
another Christmas
we staged and struck, annual ceremony
to suspend our disbelief awhile.

We carried this tree home
triumphant, hung it with coloured
balls, candy, swags
all our totem stuff
                    and we said
it would live forever
in our hearts – this needleless
tinsel-tarted up sham of a tree.

Out of pity for the dead
we should take it back
to the forest where we felled it
and nailed the cross-stand to it
                    where it was alive.
We could go there in summer
bring our poems, decorate
the sky with word-kites
catch at the stratosphere
          from that place.

75

THE SPRING-MAD SPARROW

He batters himself, flutters, against the glass
He is only flying at another male sparrow
he sees there – a spring ritual.

Yes but he wakes me up against his panic
into heart-fluttering and his beak inside
my head. I am his reflection, urgent
instinctual. Get out. Get me out.

Sunday morning Sparrow was trying to wake me
into another dimension but I fell into
the day like a kid missing a stepping stone,
falling into the stream – fun, 'scary'
                    the panic undertow – got to
get out. Let me out.

It's too small here – prophecy and memory
wing-folded against my present moment,
the person I will be aches inside
                    the cracking-shell skull
the high blue sky
I want to get out through my eyes, windows –
and a sparrow is at my window.

That's what spring is – a mad sparrow.

76

OLD FRIEND TELEPHONING

Her voice is low   slow   hopeless,
husky with hours of crying.
She says there is no one
who has room for her –
sisters and brother – her mother
hardly recognizes her.

She has decided to live with me. She
asks if my children have left
home yet, if I am free
to look after her. I say,
'No'
as gently as
her whispers allow, that they
are at home. She remembers
then that I have a husband still.

Years ago when she was
young and rich, an elegant scatterbrain
seeing a 'shrink', she asked
me how I could live with a man –
that is, without privacy, unable
to close the door after a date.
The best part of any evening was the
closing of that damn door.
'Good-night.'
I said, 'Good-night.'

77

Hurried steps, alarms, muffled
voices, whispered strategies,
plots, intrigues
in the corridor are found out –
suddenly –
scuffling. Nothing, someone
else sighs into my pillow.
I have sunk down
inside the hospital from inside
myself. I know this place. My mother
died here
in these night-dim walls of
needling, crepe-soled
nurses.

I have remembered everything,
searched the rooms – not unnoticed –
infra-red membrane walls catch my
thought-shadow
offices, kitchen, heating plant,
I ghost-cell among white-coat workers
double-shifting to restore
the damage. It was deep, the cellar
collapsed, was jacked up
on steel supports, nerve cables
rejoined and muffled
by some drug into
distant storms roaring in the ocean
cable, quiet screaming, deaf ears.
Debris is everywhere,
dead cells, red
dust, hope.

I know this place.

REGRETS ONLY

So
you want to see me.
I want the sound structure
of your voice around
me

I want to sing you
my life again –
my small antiphon –

but I am afraid of
stumbling into the old
barb-wired psycho-socio
entanglements

          like you remembering you
loved me – it seems like love
now   when even among
women love
is possible   at least not
unnatural.

We spent an afternoon together
because
your father was dead   I
was sent to comfort
you, because my mother
had died. It was too soon
so I told you what I
                thought poetry was
                              about

79

told you a song
about an old Scottish king, about
dying   and your tears
were the beginning
of my poem.

And poetry is about dying and
things going wrong – hope,
and regrets

80

CIRCE

Circe wasn't so great a sorceress.
She made pigs out of a few sailors – she
was smart enough to see
them for what they
were.

Not just that
boys will be boys, or, you know what sailors
are.
She got those sailors
right on.

PIGS.

Circe was a poet. She
could only call 'right' names and was
otherwise powerless. Is there another
power?
Stories like that come down as sorcery
because
women that clever must be witches.

Circe could not have made out Odysseus'
men as leopards or lambs,
or even as
loving and compassionate
men. That's another magic.

We all know what the sailors
would have made
out of her and her sirens if
she hadn't named them
first.

some thought it was real

NOVEMBER LEGACY

Windowed against the fallen garden waiting for
    snow,   your damn Christmas cactus
burst out its red flowers   into my mourning
you. My self-pity, decent, grey poverty against your
    cavalier gesture
the casual extravagance of your
life ended. Death
is
a
time
of wringing of hands, of
wanting
something so true that –
but no one says those things.
Or,
something to become clear along the edge of another
story – sad tales about the deaths of things –
unravelling our interwoven
nerve-ends, extricating fragments
wanting –
Midnight till morning
restless   unremembered
dreams leave a guilt and anger residue
the day's dry-wrung hands, the
tearless watching, now tears
flood out because the cactus burst out
'life goes on', trite hall-marking lie.
But
I have of you
love
left over after
twenty years cultivation
this explosion of red   refracted through the
bleak trees by my sudden tears,
a
way of seeing.

she couldn't remember going home